13 Past Midnight

Volume 1

Steve Stockton

FREE REIGN

ISBN 13: 978-1-953462-89-3

Free Reign Publishing, LLC
San Diego, CA

Contents

Introduction

In the stillness of the night, when the world seems to have halted its buzz and shadows merge with the silence, there exists a fragile boundary between the realm of the living and the mysteries of the unknown. At precisely thirteen minutes past midnight, this boundary is at its thinnest, and the tales that arise from this haunted hour are ones that have been whispered through generations, chilling the bravest souls and questioning the fabric of our reality.

Welcome to 13 Past Midnight, a collection of books that delve deep into personal encounters with the eerie, the inexplicable, and the downright terrifying. These aren't just stories – they're intimate confessions of people who've been touched by the paranormal, who've gazed into the abyss and returned to share their harrowing experiences. From shadowy figures that vanish into the night to voices that echo from empty rooms, each tale is a testament to the world beyond our own, a world that exists, whether we believe in it or not.

This series is not for the faint-hearted. It's for those who, by the glow of a single candle, dare to explore the uncharted territories of the supernatural. It's for those who crave to know what lurks in the darkness, just beyond the reach of our understanding.

So, if you've ever felt that unsettling prickling on the back of your neck, or witnessed something you couldn't quite explain in the pale moonlight, join us on this journey. Turn the page, and step into a world where every tick of the clock brings you closer to the spine-chilling reality of 13 Past Midnight.

Introduction

Steve Stockton

Chapter 1

The Terror of Elmsworth Forest

I've always been drawn to the mysterious and eerie. By age five, I was immersed in tales of the supernatural, much to my parents' amusement. They would chuckle and shield my eyes during the spooky scenes. Throughout school, I took a filmmaking class where each project I presented had an eerie twist, so much so that my teacher once commented that I should explore other genres. The reason I share this background is to emphasize my unquenchable thirst for the supernatural, a thirst that would lead me to a spine-chilling experience I'd never forget.

In Elmsworth, a town I grew up in, whispered

tales spoke of an age-old sorceress who once roamed our forests. Legend has it that she placed a curse on Elmsworth's land after being executed in the 1700s. Although many towns boasted similar tales, our legend was fortified by old documents I stumbled upon in our local library during the late 90s, long before online searches were commonplace.

In my mid-twenties, with a gap year before university and a casual job at my aunt's store, I had time to spare. Emboldened by these findings, I decided to venture into Elmsworth Forest, hoping to encounter this legendary sorceress. While my friends declined the invite, citing concerns about the forest's restricted access, my then-girlfriend, although not a fan of anything spooky, suggested I remain respectful if I attempted any spiritual communication.

In those times, our knowledge of spiritual mediums was limited. Ouija boards, marketed as amusing board games, were easily accessible, so I took one with me into the forest. To avoid detection, a friend dropped me at a trailhead after sunset, planning to pick me up at dawn.

The forest's foreboding atmosphere intensified as night deepened. Setting up camp, I eagerly awaited midnight, the supposed witching hour. Lighting a solitary candle, I placed my fingers on the Ouija board's planchette. Instantaneously, it hurtled across the board, spelling "LEAVE" repeatedly. Before I could react, it ended with a haunting message: "you belong here" and abruptly moved to "Goodbye". The candle extinguished. An oppressive sensation gripped me, and distant screams echoed eerily.

Frantically, I packed the board and ventured down a trail, attempting to distance myself. But those harrowing screams persisted. The ominous sensation intensified, and at one point, I awoke from a terrifying dream to find myself face to face with a ghastly figure.

She floated eerily, her sagging, ancient face mere inches from mine. With grotesquely angled neck and predatory eyes, she was the embodiment of horror. Her image matched the library sketches of the sorceress of yore. Around her, shadowy figures lurked, their presence felt more than seen. A primal fear consumed me. I bolted, leaving my belongings, the shadow entities and the sorceress pursuing relentlessly.

Reaching the road bordering the forest, it became evident she couldn't cross, confined by some ancient rule or curse. She watched from the trees as I hitched a ride home, her sinister shadow companions' red eyes piercing through the night.

Days later, visiting the library, I confirmed her resemblance with the sorceress in the sketches. That nightmarish ordeal forever distanced me from the supernatural. The shadow entities seem to have followed me from the forest, appearing occasionally in my life. Dreams of that night still haunt me, serving as a chilling reminder of the dangers lurking in the unknown. If sharing my tale deters even one person from meddling with forces beyond our understanding, then it's worth recounting.

Chapter 2
The Doll

It was April 6th, 1982, when we buried Kelly and it was the darkest day of my life. I watched as my sweet seven-year-old daughter's tiny casket was lowered into the cold, unforgiving ground. The tears had long since dried on my cheeks; all I felt was a hollow emptiness in my soul. It was an accident while she was riding her bike and the only blessing here was that it was quick and painless. Or at least that's what the medical examiner had told me. I was a single mother, and we were all we had in this world and now, I was more alone than ever. No words or gestures could help soothe the deep ache I had in my heart.

The weeks after her death crawled by in a haze of grief. I remember just staring at her door, knowing that her sheets were left rumbled in the rush of the morning and her pink curtains were ruffled by the small crack in the window she insisted on having open on these spring nights. I left Kelly's bedroom untouched, not having the heart to pack up her belongings. Her favorite dolls and stuffed animals still lay strewn across her bed and floor, traces of the happy little girl who once played there. Packing it up would mean that her death was final and that would be the last of her to go.

At night, I lay awake in bed, tears flowing freely as I stared at the empty darkness. A chasm inside my heart seem to yawn at the mere realization that she was no longer by my side or asking for orange juice in the mornings. Occasional creaks and groans of the old house echoed the loneliness I felt without Kelly's joyful presence. Exhaustion eventually overtook me, but there was no peace, even in sleep. My dreams were filled with Kelly calling out to me, lost and afraid. But no matter how hard I searched; I could not find her. I got to the point where I would stay awake for days, but sleep would always win one way or another.

The apparitions continued to haunt me. One night, I jolted awake, certain I heard three light taps at my bedroom window. I rushed to look outside, but saw only the moonlit yard, empty and still. The next evening, odd thumping noises seemed to drift down the hallway from Kelly's room. For hours, I lay stiffly in my bed, listening intently until the sounds faded. Over the next few weeks, the bizarre occurrences escalated. I often heard floorboards creaking and low whispers emanating from Kelly's vacant room. Though unsettled, I still could not bring myself to enter. Late one evening, a sound I could not ignore finally beckoned—the soft, unmistakable cries of Kelly's favorite baby doll. Muffy.

That doll's muffled sobs echoed through the empty house for hours on end. Initially I covered my ears and squeezed my eyes shut, willing the anguished sounds to stop. But eventually I could avoid Kelly's room no longer. Hands trembling, I turned the doorknob and slowly pushed the door open. The room was just as Kelly had left it; toys strewn across the floor in mid-play. I searched for the source of the cries until I found the doll lying atop Kelly's unmade bed. I reached for the doll with quivering hands to remove its batteries, desperate for the haunting cries to cease. As I grasped its cold plastic body, the wailing stopped abruptly. An icy chill ran down my spine. I dropped the doll and fled from the room, slamming the door sharply behind me. I didn't even look behind me lest the shadows reach out to capture me.

That night I hardly slept, shaken by the doll's actions. As daylight crept into my bedroom, I tried convincing myself it was merely a faulty toy triggering my grief and imagination. But my mind could not be so easily soothed. I had nearly drifted off to sleep when a tugging on my blankets jolted me awake. Disoriented, I lay still beneath the covers, heart pounding. Had I imagined the sensation? My exhaustion had finally won over my body's will. Lost somewhere between dreaming and wakefulness, something in the room seemed to shift. A few moments later, a small hand gently grasped my arm. It was cold but familiar. My breath caught in my throat as a familiar little voice spoke out from the darkness.

"Mama, I had a bad dream. Can I sleep in your bed?"

I froze in disbelief and shock. Kelly's sweet, soft voice was unmistakable. Tears welled up in my eyes as my heart ached to hold her. "Yes baby, come to Mama," I finally choked out. I wanted nothing more than this dream to go on forever if that meant that I could hold my baby one more time. The covers lifted and the mattress sank slightly as Kelly's slight form crawled into bed. "I'm so cold, Mama," she murmured as she huddled close to me. I wrapped my arms tightly around her, alarmed at how icy her skin felt against mine. I held her tightly and rubbed my hands roughly over her arms and then settled for holding her. "Don't worry sweetheart, Mama will keep you warm," I whispered through trembling lips. I held Kelly close, stroking her fine hair as her breathing slowed into sleep. The dream turned to darkness, and I was finally able to rest peacefully. As I began to doze, I heard a faint, "Goodnight Mama, I love you."

"I love you too, baby," I mumbled groggily, savoring this bittersweet moment with my darling daughter. Eventually I drifted off, Kelly's fragile body still cradled in my arms. Morning sunlight stirred me awake. As consciousness returned, the previous night's events seemed like a distant dream. Had it been real or just a manifestation of my intense longing for Kelly? I reached across the bed, expecting to find it cold and empty. Instead, my hand met the soft cotton of Kelly's nightgown. My heart leaped as I quickly turned to look at her.

But the joy curdled into horror as I pulled back the covers. Next to me was not my daughter, but a filthy stain of dirt, grime, and some foul green ooze. I screamed in shock and revulsion, stumbling backwards off the bed. My eyes darted around the room wildly, taking in the muddy footsteps trailing from the window to the bed. Kelly's nightgown lay crumpled and soiled at the foot of the bed. Trembling uncontrollably, I sank to the floor and wept bitterly. My longing had manifested as a cruel torment. But nothing could possibly hurt more than knowing my darling Kelly was still gone forever, and the cold emptiness inside me would remain.

Chapter 3

Eyes in the Shadowed Grove

During my years at university in 2005, I pursued my passion at the esteemed Seattle Film Institute, aiming to achieve a PhD in Cinematography. My obsession with lenses, both for recording videos and capturing stills, was evident to anyone who knew me. The era of bulky camcorders had waned, but they still held a nostalgic place in my heart. Without the convenience of today's digital devices, we had to rely on intricate film rolls and manual camera settings.

This passion was what brought me to a dense, secluded forest in Washington for a week. My dissertation involved producing a short film, the nitty-gritty details of which would probably bore you. I was fortunate to have supportive friends willing to assist, but I bore the responsibility for the primary groundwork. My love for horror inspired me to create a spine-chilling masterpiece. I managed to rent a few camping trailers at a student discount, thanks to a family connection. With all my equipment and these campers, we ventured deep into the most intimidating forest in the region. A couple of friends drove the trailers in with me and would return later.

Rumors had it that the forest hid spirits from ancient Native American legends. It was untouched and distant from civilization. I couldn't find any ownership signs, which led me to believe it was public land. Previous visits had shown me that campers frequented the spot. Some had shared eerie experiences, which I considered integrating into my film. My enthusiasm was palpable.

However, upon our arrival, an unexpected downpour commenced. Odd, given that weather forecasts had predicted clear skies for days. The majority of my crew would be joining me later, but those who came to help with the setup wished me well and promised to return in a couple of days. I decided to use the rainy interlude for b-roll footage and concept refinement.

With rain lashing around, I decided to explore the surroundings. The overcast skies, coupled with the relentless rain, amplified the eeriness of the place. Alone in such an expansive wilderness, I felt both exhilaration and unease.

After wandering for a while, a prickling sensation hinted at another presence. A low rumbling growl resonated in the air. I tried to dismiss it as my imagination, hurrying back to the relative security of the trailer. As darkness began to blanket the forest, I felt disoriented.

Fear was an undeniable companion now, but canceling the film shoot wasn't an option. The growls grew louder, seemingly pursuing me. Trying to debunk it, I scoured the vicinity with my flashlight. Briefly, the noises ceased, and I began my retreat to the camper. But then, a deep, ragged breathing filled the air.

Confronting the sound, I was met with two piercing crimson eyes, elevated almost ten feet above the ground. My mind raced, trying to identify a rational explanation. As the being stepped forth, moonlight illuminated a massive, furry creature with patches of dark and light fur. Its elongated limbs hinted at both power and agility, with extremities resembling a grotesque mix of human and beast.

Its gaze held me captive, instilling both terror and a sense of reverence. Intuitively, I felt its presence was linked to the forest's guardian spirits. A deep, huffing sound from the creature broke our stare-down.

I gestured peacefully but made a tactical retreat, fully expecting to be chased. But it simply observed. Reaching my camper, inspiration struck. Using this uncanny encounter, I revised my script, breathing new life into it. But the night wasn't over. The sound of claws scratching my camper's sides and the door handle jiggling were nerve-wracking.

Ensuring everything was locked, I took refuge in my bed. The van intermittently rocked, hinting at multiple entities outside. Hours later, the disturbances ceased, and sporadic howls were my only companions. The next day, I beckoned some crew members to accompany me. While they were puzzled by the sudden script changes, they complied. Our week culminated successfully, though I did capture a scene with those same haunting red eyes lurking in the background.

I never disclosed my encounter, choosing instead to channel the experience into my work. My writings, a blend of horror and reality, drew significant attention. I often consider revealing the true inspiration behind my first best-seller, which I've passed off as a second-hand tale. The forest left me enriched with experiences and knowledge. While I've not faced such phenomena again, I remain a believer, continually searching for the inexplicable.

Chapter 4
It Came at Night

I loved having a cabin by the lake in addition to my house in the suburbs. I grew up in a very rural area and the lake house always reminded me of home. I was lucky in that I got a job at a major corporation right out of college and was able to quickly work my way up to the point where I was making a tremendous amount of money every year by the time I was thirty. I met my husband at my job when I was just getting started and he was about ten years older than me and already established and we were able to provide a lot of luxuries to our kids. However, by the time the kids got older they were no longer interested in summers at the lake and would only want to go for a week or two at a time. One year my husband took all the kids on a trip somewhere else, I don't remember where, but I had decided to write a book, which had been a lifelong dream, and thought it would be the perfect opportunity to go to the lake house alone and spend a few weeks in peace and quiet there. I had never been there alone for any length of time, not even a whole night, and was looking forward to relaxing in my office there. The lake community was one that wrapped around the lake in a circle and was then surrounded by a dense forest, of which there was only one road that led both in and out. I arrived late the first night because it's an eight-hour drive away from our main house and I left a little late because I had been cleaning up and arranging with the neighbors to take in my mail and feed our cats while we were gone. My husband and the kids would be home before me and so we decided they should just come to the lake house and spend a weekend before we all went home together.

I stopped and picked up some groceries for the lake house and when I got there I noticed none of the neighbors seemed to be home. I didn't see any lights on or cars in their driveway and when I went out onto the back deck to look out over the lake and enjoy the sight of the full moon shining off it, I didn't see a light on in a single house. There were about twelve houses altogether in the little community and it seemed like I was a little earlier than everyone else but I was perfectly okay with that. Throughout the years my family and I had made friends with everyone in the development but I didn't really feel like gossiping with the ladies or entertaining anyone at that point in time. I was serious about starting my writing career and I knew it would be a lot easier without all the distractions of everyone stopping in to say hello and welcoming me for the season. By the time my family got there with me there should have been some other people there. I took a hot shower and went to bed. Immediately when I laid down and turned off all the lights that there was something strange happening. I felt like I was being watched despite knowing I was the only one there. I tried my best to ignore the feeling and fell asleep rather quickly. I woke up at around three in the morning to use the bathroom and the feeling of being watched was so over-whelming that after going to the bathroom I went through the entire house, turning the lights on in every single room and making sure no one was in the closets. I even opened the front and back doors with the chains on them to look out and make sure no one was outside either. After turning all the lights off and going back into my bedroom, which was in the back of the house and overlooked the lake, I still felt like someone was there with me or at the very least watching me. It was so quiet outside, which was abnormal in and of itself, that I felt like I would have been able to hear if someone was out there. I couldn't hear anything at all, which was also strange because we are surrounded by a usually loud forest and it's those noises that normally helped me to go to sleep. I curled up in my blankets and closed my eyes, trying to ignore the feeling once again. It took me about twenty minutes before I started to fall asleep again and the minute I did there was a sound coming from outside like nails scraping across my bedroom window. I jumped up and looked but there was nothing there. My bedroom in the lake house is on the second floor, so there couldn't have been anyone out there anyway. There were also no trees though and therefore I couldn't have been mistaking the noise of a tree branch scraping against the house for something scratching against the window.

I rolled over in bed so I was facing the window and kept my eyes squinted just enough to where I could see out of them but so that it looked like they were closed. I don't know what made me think to do that but I did believe in the paranormal at the time so maybe that was why. Maybe it was that I thought someone was throwing pebbles or something at the window as the development did have some trouble making teens in one of the homes across the lake from me. Eventually my eyes closed for good and I started, once again, to fall asleep. There was a loud knocking at my window, the same one where I had heard the scraping sounds a little while earlier and so I squinted my eyes open again so that if there was someone there, somehow, they would have a harder time noticing I was looking at them. I feel like my guides or my angels or something were compelling me to do that that night because like I said I honestly don't know what I was expecting to see or who I was expecting to be there with the window being on the second floor. I never expected to see what was there, looking right back at me and grinning, though. I screamed and jumped up, running to turn the light in the room on. Once the light was on and I looked back at the window, my body shaking, my heart pounding and breathing to the point where I was almost hyperventilating, of course there was nothing there anymore. I knew what I had seen though, of that there was no doubt. I saw a red faced, demonic looking creature, complete with black horns on each side of its red and round head, a hooked nose, two very large ears, a black, grinning mouth that was full of yellow and green, broken, razor sharp teeth and dark black eyes with no whites, that made me feel like for that split second I was about to lose my own soul. I flipped the light switch and turned it off and the face was there again. As soon as it was on again, the face was gone. I left the light on and sat at the edge of my bed with my head in my hands, crying and trying to understand what was happening. I heard a loud splash in the lake and ran to the other window in my bedroom to look out of it and see what was going on. All I saw were the aftereffects of something huge having gone into the lake.

I turned on all the lights in the house again and made myself a cup of tea. I was terrified but I didn't know what to do. It was around five in the morning when I finally had convinced myself that there wasn't anything out there and that either my mind had been playing tricks on me or I had still been sleeping and having a nightmare when I saw the face. As soon as those thoughts crossed my mind I heard stomping up the stairs to my back door, which was right off the lake and separated from it by only a few stone steps that came up from the dock and to my door. I froze and didn't know what to do. I also heard sloshing sounds, sort of like when someone is walking in puddles. I ran around the house as fast as I could trying to turn off all the lights and after sitting there for a few minutes I didn't hear anything. I put my ear to the back door and listened but again heard nothing. I decided to face my fears because I was starting to think that I was either going crazy or those kids from across the lake were messing with me. I really thought that it was the kids and so I swallowed my fear as best as I could and opened the back door. I marched out there and looked all around to see who was messing with me. I immediately stepped in a small puddle and there were more than a few of them, obviously footprints coming up from the dock and leading right to the front door. They weren't human footprints though and they weren't sneaker prints either. They looked like they belonged to some sort of animal that I had never seen before or that I had never noticed the feet before. They were huge and looked like they ended in three separate talons instead of toes. I had enough! I marched down the steps calling out the names of the kids from across the way but no one responded. I walked all the way around the house and my motion lights went off. It occurred to me the motion sensor lights hadn't gone off when I had seen the face in the window or when someone had walked up my steps and onto my porch. As soon as I got to the back of the house and onto the small patch of grass that was next to the stairs and that was my yard, I heard another incredibly loud splash in the lake. I looked up and that's when I saw the evil thing, in all its glory, just hovering there in the moonlight.

It was around seven feet tall and had red skin, as I described before. Its body shape looked like that of a human being but every-thing was so much bigger. It had giant muscles but the arms looked deformed and bent backwards, and it had black bat wings sprouted behind it as it hovered there over the lake in the moonlight. It was hovering about fifty feet on top of the lake and it was staring right at me, grinning with those horrible teeth. I screamed and it started flying towards me. I saw it had disgusting feet, with three gigantic talons with even more extraordinarily large nails coming off or growing out of each one. Its hands looked the same as the feet, only a little bit smaller. I could see the nose more clearly then and noticed it was more of a beak than a hooked shape as I had originally observed. Its giant wings spanned eleven feet or more across both. It swooped down and I moved out of the way, ducking under the stairs to try and keep myself safe. It made several more attempts to get to me after that but eventually it seemed like it knew it couldn't reach me and I watched as it flew off into the night, into the forest, leaving behind the echo of the animalistic yet somewhat human sounding growl it had made when it realized it couldn't take me with it. I ran as fast as I could from under the stairs and back into my house just as the sun started rising. I was terrified but couldn't get my husband or any of the kids on the phone. When I finally did tell him what was going on and what had happened to me, he laughed and told me to stop joking before I scared the kids into never wanting to go there again. I was so furious that I hung up on him and just laid in bed crying, going in and out of a restless sleep all day long, having nightmares the whole time about the beast from the woods and the lake. I knew what happened to me was real but I researched it in private because I didn't think that I could take my husband and kids making fun of the terrifying experience I had that night. I never saw the creature again and thought it came from the forest. It might have chosen that night because I was the only one there in the development and it knew no one would have been around to hear me scream. I haven't spent much time at the lake house since then but we still own it and go sometimes, but not nearly as much as we used to. I think it was a demon who not only fed off my terror and fear but was looking to take me back into the forest with it for whatever reason and luckily for me, it was thwarted.

Chapter 5

Terror on Larchmont Lane

Moving into the antiquated house on Larchmont Lane, my family was overcome with an elated sense of starting anew. Its towering facade, interwoven with ivy, spoke of an era long past. The sprawling garden, the vintage stained glass windows, everything about it felt like a dream. But dreams, as I was to discover, can swiftly turn into nightmares.

In the early days, a shroud of oddity began to settle. Items began mysteriously relocating. My great-grandfather's cherished pocket watch, once kept securely in my study, would surface in the children's toy box. My daughter's favorite necklace found its way into a kitchen jar. Even simple items, like books or pens, seemed to play a constant game of hide and seek.

But these mysterious relocations paled in comparison to the eerie figures that began to haunt the peripheries of our vision. These weren't mere illusions or tricks of the light. Once, while passing the grand mirror in the hallway, I saw a reflection not of myself but of a tall, gaunt man, standing silently, watching. Another time, my wife felt the cold touch of a hand brushing against hers, only to find no one nearby. Our home seemed to pulse with a life of its own.

The malevolence escalated. Loud bangs echoed through hallways with no discernible source. The children's room became a hotspot for activity. I would wake up to their shrill cries, dashing to their side to find their room ice cold, and their blankets and pillows strewn across the floor as if yanked away by unseen hands. The terror in their eyes was unmistakable.

The final, harrowing incident was what made

us reconsider our stay. Returning home one evening, I found my wife sitting on the stairs, her face a canvas of fear and shock. Rolling up her sleeves, she revealed dark, hand-shaped bruises encircling her arms. She recounted how an invisible entity had gripped her, shaking her violently. It was a physical manifestation of the house's malevolent intent.

Desperate for answers, I dived into the local archives, seeking out any scrap of history about our cursed residence. My search led to a gruesome discovery. Forty years prior, a brutal murder had stained the house's legacy. A man, driven to insanity, had taken the life of his entire family in a fit of rage. As I pieced together the newspaper clippings, old photographs, and whispered town tales, the horrifying truth became clear: the spirits trapped in our home sought to communicate their pain, anger, and torment.

We left the house on Larchmont Lane with haste, leaving behind more than just possessions – we left a piece of our souls. The residence stands there still, a silent sentinel to its tragic past, waiting for its next occupants. And while we've moved miles away, the memories linger, a chilling testament to the house's macabre history and the souls that remain tethered to it.

Chapter 6
The Haunting of Evergreen Estate

When I was a younger woman, an incident irrevocably shifted my perspective. Back then, my worldview was entrenched in reason, logic, and skepticism. Ghosts, spirits, or anything ethereal were mere myths to me. In those days, freshly graduated and struggling to find my place in the world, I often undertook various renovation tasks to make ends meet.

One summer day, a certain Mr. Jenkins, an acquaintance from the coastal town of Shellhaven, approached me with an intriguing proposal. He owned an old estate called Evergreen in the heart of Blackwood Forest, and it required significant refurbishment. Offering me a hefty sum, he requested I oversee and complete the project by the first snowfall of winter. Eager for the financial respite, I agreed.

Little did I know, the word "remote" hardly did justice to Evergreen's location. It wasn't just situated in the forest, it seemed to be swallowed by it. Miles from civilization, the house stood solemnly amidst nature's over-powering embrace. While initially taken aback by its isolation, the solitude felt like a welcome escape. In no time, Evergreen felt like home.

Days turned into weeks, and I grew fond of evening treks through the forest. The serenity of the twilight hours in the woods was unparal-leled. However, one evening, having been frus-trated with delivery delays and faulty materials, I sought refuge in the forest's embrace.

Walking under the canopy of stars, the night around me changed abruptly. An uncanny magenta burst illuminated the sky, not like any lightning I'd ever seen. A profound unease settled in the air post the phenomenon, transforming the previously tranquil woods into a shadowy realm of foreboding.

Chilling whispers seemed to dance on the wind as I felt unseen eyes watch me. A smaller magenta flicker, like a rogue firefly, caught my attention. Before I could process it, the light coalesced into a towering shadowy apparition, donned with a classic trilby and glowing pink eyes — starkly contrasting the typical red-eyed specters one reads about.

As the silhouette leaned against a nearby oak, the environment turned chaotic. Gusts howled, and the celestial lights vanished as if cloaked by an unseen hand. Not wanting to give in to panic, I hastened my steps, haunted by phantom grimaces emerging from the trees and an ominous presence close behind.

Upon reaching Evergreen, I secured every possible entry, the echo of ethereal lamentations and relentless pounding echoing around. Exhausted and overwhelmed, I collapsed into bed, only to be met with a series of tormenting dreams. One, particularly vivid, involved a mesmerizing woman with those same piercing magenta eyes, who, in a sinister twist, revealed her malevolent, demonic form, dragging me by my feet and marking me with her claws.

The morning sun dispelled the night's horrors, but the scars of the ordeal were palpable – three distinct scratches ran down my back, and hand-shaped bruises marked my ankles.

Though the mansion renovations concluded timely, the spectral entity did not limit itself to Blackwood Forest. Even now, years later, I occasionally glimpse those haunting pink eyes from dark corners and wake up to inexplicable injuries. I've kept this tale locked away, fearing ridicule or worse, institutionalization. Yet, sharing it now feels like a weight lifting, even if the entity's shadow lingers.

Publisher's Excerpt 1

FEAR IN THE FOREST: VOLUME 1

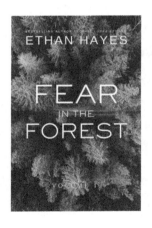

ANGRY SPIRITS FROM THE WOODS

I inherited a cabin that belonged to my grandparents when I was twenty eight years old. It was a shock as they both died tragically, suddenly and together but also because no one knew they even owned a cabin. We are from the northeastern part of the United States and that's where most of my family was born and raised and where most of them still reside to this day. So, it was shocking when the will was read and I was told I had inherited a large chunk of money and a rustic, old cabin in the middle of the woods in Colorado. I was excited and couldn't have been more pleased. I could certainly use the money at the time even though I was unmarried and didn't have any kids yet. It afforded me the opportunity to be able to do some things I had always wanted to do but that I had been putting off in the rat race that is the corporate world where I worked. I broke the lease on my tiny apartment in the city, bought myself an old and used camper-van, stuffed it full of my belongings and headed out to Colorado within a week of inheriting the cabin. I had a job where I mainly worked from home but I took a few weeks off anyway because I wanted to be able to settle in and have some peace and quiet to myself. I was always very close with my grandparents, being the only grandchild, and though I was devastated at the loss, I felt so grateful to them for looking out for me the way that they had. My parents weren't happy about my moving to Colorado on what they called "a whim" but I knew it was the right thing for me to do at that time. Personally I just think they were jealous I was left a lot more than they were but I never would have said that to their faces. I promised my mother that as soon as I got settled in I would let her know and then if they wanted to they could come and check out the cabin. She settled for that much and I left without ever planning on looking back.

I had no idea how far out into the sticks the cabin was. I figured it would be fairly isolated given how my grandparents always valued their privacy but I got quite a shock when I spent a half hour's time driving on three separate, country, back roads, each! It was literally in the middle of nowhere and in the middle of the woods. I was definitely not used to being out in the country and had never been camping, hunting, hiking or anything like that my entire life. I had always wanted to do those things and I figured there was no time like the present. What I hadn't been told was that the cabin they owned was a part of an old summer camp that shut down in the sixties and they sold off the cabins one by one to the highest bidders. To me that was crazy but it ended up being pretty cool. I had neighbors, somewhere around in between all the trees and other woods and there was a huge lake in the compound as well. I didn't see any other cabins on the drive into the place and I hadn't even seen a gas station in the last twenty miles or so but I knew there had to have been other people there, especially at that time of year. It was the end of fall and winter was just starting to rear its ugly head. I knew it snowed a lot in Colorado but that wasn't anything I was used to, or so I thought, having lived in a big city on the northeastern seaboard my whole life. I had no clue what I was in for, and not only with the weather either. It didn't take long for me to get my first dose of the terrifying and the supernatural things that came from those woods and had, somehow and at some point, become a part of that cabin and everything around it.

I had to bring in some professionals to do small jobs on various parts of the building and land but it was all very minor things and initial inspections, stuff like that. They were all local companies I had found in the yellow pages. It was odd though that when I would answer the door they would always take a step back and every single one of them refused my offer to come inside and warm up for a minute before or after doing what they needed to do. Finally one of them, a woman who had to come in to make sure all of my wires and things were up to date, flat out said, "There's no way I'm going in there so please be honest and answer the questions I'm about to ask you."

I thought it was kind of rude and blatantly explained that my cabin was said to be haunted and all types of crazy things had been seen and heard coming from there, mainly at night throughout the course of all the years since the camp closed down. While she refused to get into any more detail she said that a few years back my grandparents had to be called out there because there were people performing rituals in there and someone had called the police and she also claimed that the tragedies there were unnatural and occurred way more than what would be considered a normal amount, starting all the way back when it was still a summer camp. She told me it was a literal portal to hell because it had been built on top of one. I was in shock and thought she was crazy. I answered her questions and couldn't have been more pleased when she was finally off my porch.

At first I noticed a lot of little, weird things happening in the cabin but nothing that alarmed me or made me feel unsafe or like I was living on top of a portal to hell. The one thing was the constant and almost obsessive banging that would happen every single night when I would lay down for bed. I would lay down and listen to my music fairly loudly on the radio because it helped me to unwind and fall asleep faster. I listened to classical music before bed but it seemed like every single time I would turn it on, there would be a strange banging sound like someone was stomping up and down on the floor right next to me but there was no one there. I heard it a lot when I was in my bedroom specifically but it was never as bad as when I was playing my music before bed. I'm gonna make a long story short here but one thing aside from the banging was a feeling like I was always being watched, not just inside of the house but outside as well. It felt like the woods had taken on a life of their own and something within them was always watching me. It was eerie and made spending time on the back deck and enjoying the beautiful view not even worth it anymore. I didn't go out there much after the first month.

Finally the time came when my parents were insisting they wanted to come and visit and so they did. It was right before the first major snowfall of the season and they got to my house just in time to end up snowed in with me. We had a good time but my mother came in one day and asked me if I had met the old woman who used to live here. I asked her what she was talking about and she said she had been on the back deck smoking a cigarette when a little old lady came up and asked her how she likes the place. My mother explained to her that she loved it and was thinking about buying one of them in the area herself. The old woman told her that she used to live in my cabin but now she lived somewhere else. The woman pointed in the direction to the back of the house and into the woods. That wasn't too worrisome or unbelievable because the other cabins were located all within the woods and throughout the area. It was very rugged and also very massive so I knew I hadn't seen all of the cabins yet despite having been there for a little over a month. The activity in the cabin was getting bad and my parents and I noticed shadow entities in the corners and they also seemed to be standing at the foot of the beds in the middle of the night but it was all chalked up to us possibly seeing things. When it came to the things that would be there one minute and gone the next like keys, the remote or even a hairbrush, we convinced ourselves that we had simply been mistaken about where we had left those items in the first place. Then one night, everything changed.

I was upstairs in my room, listening to my classical music and getting ready for bed when the banging started. There was an empty bedroom in the room below me where I had one bed and the rest of my boxes I still had to unpack. Across from that room, on the ground floor was the guest room where my parents were staying. The banging was so loud I went downstairs and asked my parents if they could hear it and they said they thought it was coming from the room across from theirs and they had been hearing it every night like I had. I think up until that point none of us wanted to accept that maybe the place was haunted. We all went into the spare room to look and see if we could figure it out but there was nothing there. As we all turned to leave something caught my eye in the mirror and I kid you not I screamed like a little girl. There, sitting on the bed directly across from the mirror was a little old lady with blazing red eyes. She had a broom in her hand and as she looked at me and smiled a terrifying and evil grin, she started slamming the broom handle into the ceiling above her. That was what the banging had been the whole time. Suddenly, as both my parents turned to look, the lady could be seen on the bed and she got up and angrily stormed towards us. She yelled in a demonic voice for us to get the hell out of her house. I didn't know what else to do so we ran from the room and I slammed the door in her face. We were in such a panic we ran out the back door and were on the deck. It was snowing like crazy.

There were footprints in the snow leading from my back deck, down the few stairs and into the woods. I thought someone had broken

in and my rational mind said the old lady was
in on it. When my mother told me it was the
same old woman she had seen that had said
she used to live there, I became furious and
thought my hillbilly neighbors were trying to
rob me. I grabbed my jacket and ran into the
woods to follow the footprints. It was dark
outside at that time but I had brought a flashlight, thank God for my mother who had
thought ahead. I shined it everywhere but
didn't see anything around me but I knew
someone was watching me the whole time. I
yelled for whoever it was to show themselves
and called them a coward and some other
choice and not so nice words. Suddenly, the
footprints stopped at the lake. I looked up but
there was no one there and other than my own
there were no footprints anywhere. That's
when I looked up and saw shadow beings with
glowing red eyes all around me, coming out
from behind the trees. They started walking
towards me and in my terror I could do nothing
but scream. They all looked startled for a
minute and I thought for a second it was me

who had somehow been able to intimidate them. They all turned their heads at the same time towards the lake, which was frozen over and snow covered. There, directly in the middle of the lake, there was a huge, black figure. It was blacker than the darkness of the night and looked like it was wearing a cloak or hood of some kind. It was at least thirteen feet tall and carried a scythe. It looked almost like the comic book and horror movie images of Death itself. And it was coming right towards me.

As the regular sized shadow beings closed in on me I took off running. I ran as fast as I could back to my house but on the way the old lady came out from behind a tree. She was almost snarling, her eyes blazing. She shook her broom at me and told me, again in the demonic voice, to get out of her house. I didn't stop and ran right into her, knocking her down into the snow in the process. She let out an ear piercing howl behind me and when I turned around she was gone. There was a huge mark in the snow though where she had fallen on the ground. I kept running but right before I got to my house, I saw that the giant shadow/Death being was standing on the stairs to the back porch. It was perfectly still and its cloak wasn't blowing in the breeze or anything. It also seemed to be completely unaffected by the snow as it remained pristine and untouched by the stuff. It pulled a pocket watch or something similar out of its pocket, looked at it, and then looked back at me. It started to walk towards me and all I could think to do was pray. I prayed fervently like I had never prayed before. When I opened my eyes it was gone but I could still feel a presence watching me from the woods. I ran inside and eventually I calmed down enough to tell my parents what happened. They believed me but there wasn't anywhere we could go. We were snowed in, in a cabin in the middle of nowhere and there was no way out. There was a state of emergency outside and in most of the state at the time so only emergency vehicles were allowed to be on the roads for any reason. We were stuck there, at least for a little while.

The activity got worse and worse as each day passed and I could write a book about everything terrifying that went on in that place. My parents and I all slept together in the living room and eventually we came to discuss why my grandparents had given me the cabin and none of us could understand it. Once the snow cleared my parents went home and begged me to go with them. I couldn't though because I loved the cabin itself and the land around it too much. I called in some specialists who deal with the paranormal and one of them was a medicine woman from a Native tribe in the area. She told me I had angered the Great Spirit in the woods and that he felt like he and I were at war. Therefore he was attacking me and sending in all of the resources available to him. She said that if I earnestly apologized and gave a peace offering, that he MIGHT allow me to stay and live there in peace. I thought it was all mumbo jumbo and thought that I was dealing with something definitely evil and from hell itself. However, I was willing to try anything at that point and so I did what she told me to do. I bought some tobacco and a small bottle of liquor and went out to the edge of the woods. I apologized with my arms out to what or whoever the Great Spirit was and suddenly, for the first time since I had been there I felt at peace. I even felt something touch my hand as though it were shaking it. The "war" was over, apparently.

I bring gifts to the Spirit at the start of every season and I still live in the cabin. I had to learn to live with the shadow beings but the huge one I thought was death hasn't shown up again since I made peace with the entity in the woods. They torment me sometimes but it's always in waves and then for a few months it'll all be quiet. I had to bring in a medium to get rid of the old lady and the rest is, as they say, history. I've contemplated just selling the place but it has a hold on me and I'm somewhat attached to it now. Also, I don't want anyone else to have to go through what I went through with the Spirit in the woods or that I still go through with the shadow beings. Since no one knows what they are or where they come from, there's really no getting rid of them. There are several documented cases where they're said to have killed people but I keep close to my faith and that's all I can do. Thanks for letting me share.

* * *

FEAR IN THE FOREST: VOLUME 1

Publisher's Excerpt 2

CONSPIRACY THEORIES THAT WERE TRUE

TUSKEGEE SYPHILIS EXPERIMENT

The Tuskegee Syphilis Experiment, also known as the Tuskegee Study of Untreated Syphilis in the Negro Male, is one of the most infamous cases of unethical human experimentation in U.S. history, and at one time was considered a conspiracy theory. The study was initially supposed to last six months but ended up continuing for 40 years, from 1932 to 1972.

ORIGINS:

The study began in 1932 in Macon County, Alabama, and was conducted by the U.S. Public Health Service (USPHS).

Dr. Taliaferro Clark was the original architect of the study. Initially, Dr. Clark intended the study to be a short-term project to record the progression of syphilis and then offer treatment. However, under subsequent leadership, the study's purpose shifted to observing the long-term effects of untreated syphilis.

KEY FIGURES / INSTITUTIONS OVER THE YEARS:

The initiation and continuation of the Tuskegee Syphilis Experiment were facilitated by a combination of institutional decisions by the USPHS, complicit actions by key individuals, and the broader societal context of racial discrimination and unequal access to health-care. The study's prolonged duration, despite clear ethical violations, is a testament to the systemic issues that allowed such an experiment to persist for four decades.

- **Dr. Raymond Vonderlehr:** He succeeded Dr. Clark and became the on-site director of the study. Under his leadership, the intention of the study was redefined to observe untreated syphilis in black males until their deaths. Vonderlehr developed the procedures for the study and was involved in its operations for many years.
- **Dr. John Heller:** He was another central figure in the study who directed it for a significant portion of its duration, particularly during the years after World War II. Under his tenure, the

withholding of treatment continued, even after penicillin was recognized as a standard and effective treatment for syphilis.

- **Dr. Oliver Wenger:** While not directly overseeing the study, Wenger was a key figure in the USPHS's venereal disease section and supported the Tuskegee experiment.

- **Tuskegee Institute:** The Tuskegee Institute (now Tuskegee University), a historically black college in Alabama, played a role in the study. The USPHS collaborated with the Institute, which provided logistical support and helped gain the trust of the local community. However, it's essential to note that the primary responsibility and decision-making authority for the study's design and continuation lay with the USPHS.

- **Dr. Eugene Dibble:** He was the head of the John Andrew Hospital at the Tuskegee Institute and was involved in the study, mainly in its early stages.

- **Eunice Rivers:** She was a black nurse who played a significant role in the day-to-day operations of the study. Rivers was responsible for maintaining contact with the participants, ensuring they attended scheduled appointments, and acted as a bridge between the researchers and the community. Because of her involvement and trust within the community, many participants stayed in the study.

MAIN FEATURES OF THE EXPERIMENT:

The study involved 600 black men, of which 399 had syphilis and 201 did not. The men were told they were being treated for "bad blood," a colloquial term used in the community to describe several ailments, including syphilis, anemia, and fatigue.

The participants were not informed of their syphilis diagnosis nor were they informed about the study's true purpose. Instead, they were told they were receiving free healthcare, meals, and burial insurance in exchange for participating.

Even when penicillin became the standard treatment for syphilis in 1947, the men in the study were neither informed about this development nor provided with the antibiotic. Researchers intentionally withheld treatment to observe the disease's progression.

DECEPTION:

There's no documented evidence that the men in the Tuskegee Syphilis Experiment were collectively aware that they were being deceived and subsequently made public claims about the study during its early years or even much of its duration. It's essential to understand the context and the level of manipulation involved:

The participants were deceived from the start. They were told that they were being treated for "bad blood," a local term that could refer to several conditions, including syphilis, anemia, and fatigue. The U.S. Public Health Service provided them with placebos, ineffective methods, and diagnostic procedures under the guise of "treatment." Because of this, many of the men believed they were receiving genuine healthcare.

Medical authorities, especially during the time when the study began, were highly respected. The men had little reason to doubt the intentions of the health professionals involved, especially when they were provided with certain benefits like free medical check-ups and meals during examinations.

Nurse Rivers played a pivotal role in maintaining the trust of the participants. As a Black nurse who was part of their community, she was instrumental in keeping the men involved in the study. Her relationship with the participants further ensured that they felt they were in good hands.

Many of the participants were not well-informed about syphilis, its treatments, or the broader implications of medical research. This lack of information, combined with the intentional deception by the study's conductors, made it less likely for the men to question the proceedings.

The racial dynamics of the American South in the early to mid-20th century meant that Black individuals often faced systemic racism, were marginalized, and lacked resources. Such a context might have made it even more challenging for the participants to voice concerns or seek second opinions.

EXPOSED:

The Tuskegee Syphilis Experiment became public knowledge in 1972. The unethical practices of the study were brought to national attention by Peter Buxtun, a former Public Health Service interviewer and whistleblower. Buxtun had expressed his concerns about the study to his superiors within the USPHS several times since the late 1960s, but it was only after no internal action was taken that he decided to go to the press.

Jean Heller, a reporter for the Associated Press, broke the story on July 25, 1972, revealing the details of the study to the general public. The article described how for four decades, the U.S. Public Health Service had deliberately withheld treatment from hundreds of black men with syphilis as part of a research experiment.

When the Tuskegee Syphilis Experiment was exposed by Jean Heller in 1972, the government did not deny the study's existence or its details. The facts were well-documented, and Peter Buxtun, the whistleblower, provided evidence about the experiment. Additionally, the U.S. Public Health Service, which had overseen the study, did not dispute the revelations once they were made public and shut it down.

However, in the immediate aftermath of the story breaking, some officials and representatives of the U.S. Public Health Service tried to justify or defend the study's intent and procedures, citing the research's importance or arguing that standards and norms had changed since the study began in 1932. This stance was not a denial but rather an attempt to provide context or justification, which was widely seen as insufficient and unsatisfactory given the gross ethical violations.

The media, for its part, generally reported on the story with shock and outrage. The revelations led to extensive media coverage, which played a crucial role in informing the public about the study's details and the ethical issues at stake.

The overwhelming negative reaction from the public, medical community, and media alike led to congressional hearings, which culminated in a stronger framework for the protection of human subjects in research studies and ultimately the creation of institutional review boards (IRBs) to oversee and approve research involving human participants.

CONSEQUENCES AND OUTCOMES:

Many participants of the study suffered severe health complications due to untreated syphilis, and some even died from the disease. Their families also suffered, with spouses becoming infected and children born with congenital syphilis.

In 1973, a $10 million out-of-court settle-
ment was reached, and the U.S. government
promised to give lifetime medical benefits and
burial services to all living participants. The
widows of the participants were also provided
with health benefits.

In 1997, President Bill Clinton formally apologized on behalf of the U.S. government to the
surviving participants of the study and their
families.

The experiment sowed deep distrust among
many in the Black community towards the U.S.
healthcare system, which still reverberates
today.

* * *

CONSPIRACY THEORIES THAT WERE TRUE

Publisher's Excerpt 3

LEGENDS AND STORIES: FROM THE APPALACHIAN TRAIL

SERIAL KILLERS ON THE TRAIL

Gary Hilton - The Appalachian Trail Predator

Gary Michael Hilton, known for his heinous crimes along the Appalachian Trail, etched a dark legacy in the early 2000s. His series of murders in the picturesque but remote wilderness sowed fear among hikers and residents in the surrounding areas. This chapter aims to delve into the life, crimes, and eventual downfall of Hilton, illuminating the shadows cast by this notorious figure.

Gary Hilton was born in November 1946. Details about his early life are sparse, but it's understood that he had a tumultuous relationship with his family and struggled socially. He served in the military during the Vietnam War, but his service was marked by disciplinary issues.

Hilton's criminal activities escalated over time. Initially involved in petty crimes, he gradually descended into more violent offenses. He was known to be a drifter, spending extensive time in the natural reserves and mountainous terrains of the Appalachian region.

One of Hilton's most infamous crimes was the kidnapping and murder of Meredith Emerson, a 24-year-old hiker, in January 2008. Emerson was hiking with her dog on Georgia's

Blood Mountain when she encountered Hilton. Witnesses last saw her in his company. After a meticulous search, Emerson's decapitated body was found, leading to Hilton's arrest. He eventually pleaded guilty to her murder and provided details about the crime, resulting in a life sentence.

Emerson was not Hilton's only victim. Authorities linked him to the murder of an elderly couple, John and Irene Bryant, who were hiking in North Carolina. Hilton was also implicated in the killing of Cheryl Dunlap in Florida. Each crime exhibited a chilling modus operandi, where the victims were abducted, tormented, and eventually killed.

Hilton's reign of terror ended with his arrest and subsequent conviction. He was sentenced to life in prison for Emerson's murder, and he received a death sentence in Florida for Dunlap's murder. His crimes sent shockwaves through the community, prompting discussions and initiatives to enhance safety measures in hiking trails and wilderness areas.

Gary Hilton's crimes left an indelible mark

on the Appalachian Trail community. His acts cast shadows over the pristine wilderness, turning the serene trails into haunting landscapes for those who remembered the tales of the Appalachian Trail Predator. In the wake of his crimes, hikers and authorities alike became more vigilant, working to ensure that the trails remained safe for all.

The Dark Journey of Randall Lee Smith

Randall Lee Smith, whose name has been etched into the sinister annals of Appalachian Trail history, was involved in a series of heinous crimes that sent shockwaves through the hiking community. His dark tale begins in 1981 when the Appalachian Trail witnessed a tragic event that would forever taint its serene wilderness.

Little is known about Randall Lee Smith's early life, as he primarily became known for the criminal activities he later engaged in. Smith was a local of Pearisburg, Virginia, living near the tranquil but treacherous terrains of the Appalachian Trail.

In May 1981, the peaceful aura of the Appalachian Trail was shattered when two hikers, Susan Ramsey and Robert Mountford Jr., were found dead near the trail in Virginia. Both had been shot and their bodies left in the dense, secluded woods, creating an atmosphere of dread and horror amongst other hikers and local residents.

Ramsey and Mountford were actively involved in social work and were trekking the trail to raise funds for a Maine special education school. Their journey, filled with hope and benevolence, met a tragic end at the hands of Smith.

Following the discovery of the bodies, an extensive investigation was launched, leading to the arrest of Randall Lee Smith. Despite the absence of a clear motive, evidence against Smith was overwhelming, resulting in his conviction. The courts sentenced him to two consecutive life sentences, but an appeal would later reduce his incarceration period.

Smith was released on parole in 1996, having served merely 15 years of his sentence. Shockingly, he would return to a life of crime, his freedom leading to another gruesome incident near the Appalachian Trail in 2008.

Smith attacked two fishermen, Scott Johnston and Sean Farmer, near the trail close to where he had committed the first set of murders. Although injured, Johnston and Farmer managed to escape, and Smith was soon apprehended by the authorities. However, fate had its own plans, as Smith died in custody, succumbing to injuries sustained during a vehicle crash while he was attempting to elude capture.

Randall Lee Smith's crimes cast a long shadow over the Appalachian Trail community, sowing seeds of fear and caution amongst those who sought solace in its serene embrace. His tale serves as a chilling reminder that danger can lurk even in the most unexpected and tranquil places.

His actions, while horrifying, are anomalies amidst the myriad of inspiring and uplifting stories that have originated from the trail over the years. The Appalachian Trail, with its majestic landscapes and the promise of adventure, continues to beckon to those seeking connection with nature and themselves, albeit with the cautionary tales of the past echoing through its misty, silent woods.

Shadows on the Trail: Paul David Crews

In the quiet, serene landscapes of the Appalachian Trail, where nature unveils its raw beauty, there lurk tales of shadowy figures that have, over time, painted certain sections of the trail with strokes of dread and fear. One such figure that haunts the annals of the trail's history is Paul David Crews, a name synonymous with a chilling double murder that unfolded in the summer of 1990.

Little is publicly known about the early life of Paul David Crews due to the limited availability of records. It is known that he hailed from Florida and had a troubled background, with various run-ins with the law. Crews was somewhat of a drifter, and by the time he reached Pennsylvania, he had a criminal record and was wanted for parole violations.

In September 1990, two hikers, Molly LaRue and Geoffrey Hood, were traversing the picturesque but challenging terrains of the Appalachian Trail. LaRue, originally from Shaker Heights, Ohio, and Hood, from Signal Mountain, Tennessee, were experienced and enthusiastic outdoor adventurers. However, the duo's fateful encounter with Crews at the Thelma Marks Shelter near Duncannon, Pennsylvania, would bring their journey to a tragic end.

LaRue and Hood were part of a community of hikers that shared a passion for exploration and adventure. They had formed bonds with fellow travelers and were well-known and respected in the hiker community. Unfortunately, their paths crossed with Crews, who, bearing a shotgun, embodied danger and malice.

On the tragic day, Crews attacked and killed

Hood, shooting him in the back with his shotgun. The motive of the attack remains uncertain, though it's speculated that robbery and Crews' unstable mental state played significant roles. After killing Hood, Crews proceeded to attack LaRue, binding her hands and killing her. The bodies of the two hikers were later found at the shelter.

The double homicide sent shockwaves through the hiker community and law enforcement agencies engaged in a manhunt to capture Crews. He was eventually apprehended while attempting to flee and was charged with the heinous crimes.

During the trial, Crews was found guilty of the murders and was sentenced to life in prison without the possibility of parole. The judgment brought some semblance of closure to the families of the victims, but the echoes of the tragedy continued to reverberate through the Appalachian Trail community.

The murders committed by Paul David Crews added a dark chapter to the history of the Appalachian Trail. This event served as a harsh reminder of the vulnerabilities hikers might face on the trail, prompting discussions and measures to improve safety for those seeking solitude and adventure in the wilderness.

The tale of Paul David Crews and the tragic events of 1990 at the Thelma Marks Shelter remain etched in the collective memory of the Appalachian Trail community. These events, while casting a long shadow, also highlight the resilience and strength of the hiker community, serving as a somber reminder to tread lightly and stay vigilant while embracing the call of the wild. The trail, with its undulating hills, dense forests, and breathtaking vistas, continues to inspire and beckon adventurers, while silently bearing witness to tales of joy, discovery, and loss.

Terror on the Trail: James Jordan

James Louis Jordan, an individual known to many on the Appalachian Trail as "Sovereign," cast a dark shadow on the iconic hiking route in 2019. His actions left the tight-knit community of trail enthusiasts shaken, highlighting the unpredictable dangers that might lurk in the most unexpected places.

Limited information is available on Jordan's early life, and much of what is known emerges from the period leading up to and during his crimes on the Appalachian Trail. It's crucial to approach such profiles with the understanding that the information might not provide a comprehensive view of the individual's life history.

James Jordan began appearing on the Appalachian Trail in early 2019. Fellow hikers and trail enthusiasts noticed his erratic and often intimidating behavior. He was known to approach camping groups menacingly, sometimes brandishing a knife, leading to several uncomfortable and threatening encounters.

Jordan was initially arrested in April 2019 after an altercation with fellow hikers on the trail. However, he was eventually released with probation, allowing him to return to the trail.

The early incidents with Jordan set a tense atmosphere among hikers, leading many to share warnings and advice on how to avoid or handle encounters with him.

In May 2019, the tensions culminated in a tragic incident near the Wythe County portion of the trail in Virginia. Jordan attacked a group of four hikers camping together for safety. He approached their camp singing and playing his guitar before threatening them. In the ensuing struggle, one hiker was injured, and another, Ronald S. Sanchez Jr., a U.S. Army veteran, was fatally stabbed.

The other hikers managed to escape, alerting authorities to the dangerous situation unfolding on the trail. It led to a swift response, with law enforcement agencies mobilizing to locate and apprehend Jordan.

James Jordan was arrested and charged with murder and assault with the intent to murder. The event sent shockwaves through the Appalachian Trail community, highlighting the unpredictability of the dangers hikers might face even from fellow travelers.

The incident prompted discussions and reflections on safety, preparedness, and community among hikers. The tragic loss of Ronald Sanchez and the terror experienced by others in the group served as a sobering reminder of the importance of vigilance and support within the hiking community.

Jordan was deemed competent to stand trial after a psychiatric evaluation, though proceedings have been delayed and drawn out. The case brought against him under-scores the delicate balance between addressing mental health issues and ensuring that justice is served for the victims and their families.

The shadow cast by James Jordan on the Appalachian Trail in 2019 is a dark chapter in the history of this beloved hiking route. The events serve as a tragic reminder of the unpre-dictability of life and the importance of community, vigilance, and preparedness when venturing into the wilderness. As the legal proceedings against Jordan continue, the hiking community remembers, reflects, and learns from the incidents, hoping to prevent similar tragedies in the future.

The stories of these four killers underscores the necessity of vigilance and preparedness when embarking on adventures in isolated areas like the Appalachian Trail. Be safe out there and maintain situational awareness at all times.

CONTINUE WITH
LEGENDS AND STORIES: FROM THE
APPALACHIAN TRAIL

Chapter 7

The Black Shadow Man

I have always been obsessed with the paranormal and I own every single horror movie that's ever come out, even some that are very obscure and that I had to pay a lot of money for. I am a collector of some allegedly haunted objects as well. However, my experiences with the paranormal didn't start until I bought an allegedly haunted house, knowing that it was haunted, back in the eighties before it was considered cool to do so. It started with my love of horror movies and a woman who lived down the street from me when I was growing up. She claimed to be a witch but most people just thought she was crazy. She wasn't mean and she didn't look like what people back then thought witches were supposed to look like and that's probably why when she made the claims that she did no one believed her. It's almost a cliche how I got to know her and started cultivating my interest in the paranormal. I was playing ball in my backyard with some of my friends one summer day and after a while, instead of playing, we were messing around more than anything. We ended up putting my baseball through the woman's window. Back then, even if your neighbor was considered strange and somewhat of an outcast in the community you were still polite and friendly to them and you still invited them to barbecue and things like that. The woman was beautiful and in her late twenties at the time. My parents lived at the end of a street which only had about ten homes on it and was surrounded by forest.

My parents had gotten to know the young woman next door who never proclaimed that she was a witch but who wasn't shy about telling anyone in the mostly Christian community that she was pagan and practiced the Wiccan religion. Again, things like that were unheard of back then and even if you did those things you kept them to yourself. We didn't have as much "satanic panic" as most small towns back in that time in this country but we had some and all of this happened before it got crazy and the woman was basically run out of the neighborhood and then out of the town. She doesn't have much to do with my story except that when my friends and I broke that window in her house, my mother made me go over and help her out with things she needed done around her house for two whole weeks, until she thought I had worked off the money for the window. She insisted that it was no problem and kids will be kids but my mother insisted in the other way and won.

The woman had things in her house I had never seen before and most of it had to do with her religion. However, she had one room that had an array of different items that didn't look like they belonged together and some of them didn't look like they belonged in the house of a young, unmarried woman such as herself. She saw my interest and taught me all about her religion and told me the items in that room were haunted. She told me not to tell anyone she was talking to me about those things and as a fourteen-year-old boy with something of a crush on her, I didn't tell anyone. I enjoyed spending time with her but I remember strange things were always happening in her house when I was there. She said that the haunted items she owned had brought a lot of restless spirits with them and that it wasn't dangerous if none of the objects ever left the house and fell into the hands of someone who didn't know how to charm them, as she put it, which basically meant keep the entities from getting out of control. The reason I bring her up aside from how she helped me to become obsessed with the para- normal and haunted objects is because the one thing she had more of than anything else were old fashioned photos. She said they were real but I wasn't sure that I believed her at the time. There were people sitting in the photos, hanging all over the walls of her home, almost in every room and in very large frames, and there was strange stuff floating all around them that looked like little clouds. The woman explained to me that it was ectoplasm which, in its simplest terms, is the energy left behind by spirits after they've been in one spot. She explained all of it to me but I will just put it like that and move on so that I can keep this short. So, I knew that the cloudy looking images hanging all around the people in the photos was the excess energy spirits left behind and that was something I never forgot. The images were creepy enough and some of them had actual spirits, shadow beings and demons in them and in those ones there was very little ectoplasm left. It seemed like the eviler the entity was, the less it left behind.

Eventually the woman moved away and I moved out on my own. I bought my own home from a friend who was desperate to get rid of it and sold it to me at a bargain because she insisted that it was haunted. I believed in those things, but I had never had anything too bizarre happen to me that I couldn't reason it away, except for in the neighbor lady's home years before. I had stayed at that friend's house and never had anything happen to me when I was there either and I was just thinking of getting a house at a steal and I took her up on the offer. I had collected a few haunted items by then as well but never investigated having anyone come by and "charm" them and I'll send you some stories about those later. Once I bought the house I had a housewarming party. It was summer and there was a pool and fire pit outside so I invited several friends over and we had a barbecue and hung out late into the night. Throughout the night though several odd things happened. I had only been living in the house for a week at that time and still wasn't even fully unpacked and the woman who I had brought it from wouldn't come to the party because she wanted nothing to do with the house anymore. We all felt watched and specifically we felt like something was watching us from the woods. I hadn't gone into the woods yet but thought it was possible, based on my personal beliefs, that there were spirits dwelling inside of them that were more than likely curious about us. You see, I didn't take it all seriously at that point and really didn't understand the dangers of acquiring allegedly haunted objects and living in an allegedly haunted home. I thought it was cool and somewhat funny. During that party I told my friends about the experiences my other friend, the one who had sold me the house and who none of them knew, had been having in the home and the reason I had bought it from her. Some of them were curious, some nervous and some laughed and thought that it was all a bunch of nonsense. We were outside having a good time but we couldn't shake the feelings of being watched and throughout the night several of my friends felt like they were hearing noises coming from the woods, being touched by unseen hands and even some of them said they heard whispering in their ears. An evil voice telling them to do horrible things to the rest of us. It was when we all saw a set of glowing red eyes looking at us from the woods that most of my guests left.

There were three of us guys left and we were cleaning up and talking about the night's events. One of them said he felt even more uncomfortable inside of the house than he had outside and he bailed as well. My best friend and I were walking through the house and I was showing him my collection of haunted items when he got the bright idea to take my Ouija board into the woods to see if we could contact what had been watching us that night. I was reluctant but he talked me into it and we went out there. I was into something new I had learned about which was spirit photography, where you snap random photos in allegedly haunted places and you are supposed to be able to catch random entities in the photos. I grabbed my camera and decided to try it out. From the moment we walked into the woods we were both scared. We knew with absolute certainty that something was watching us and whatever it was, it didn't want us out there. We were encroaching on its territory and after taking several photos as we walked, I got the distinct feeling that we needed to turn around and leave. My friend, who had thought it was all so hilarious at first, looked more freaked out than I was and told me he felt the exact same way; like something was warning us to get the hell out of there and not come back. We were walking back to my house and suddenly my friend was shoved from behind so hard that he went flying forwards and landed on his face. We heard loud and terrifying growling sounds coming from behind us and without looking back, he and I got the hell out of there. We ran and he didn't stop until he was inside my house. I stopped at the tree line and snapped several photos. I felt a random gust of wind that seemed to have come out of nowhere that almost knocked me down and heard the words "get out" growling into my head. I turned and ran into the house. I checked on my friend and asked if he was okay. Aside from a bloody nose he was fine and I took pictures of his face like that, though I'm not sure why I did so. He left and that was it for the night. After that experience in the forest the activity in the house became violent and extremely dangerous but that's not what I am writing about this time. I chose to write this story because it was insane just how many spirits had been with us that night. I'll tell you how I know.

About a week later I got the photos developed from the party. Not just the ones I took while I was in the woods with my friend but the ones from the party itself, when everyone was still having a good time and having fun. In every single picture there was a huge, very tall, black shadow figure with red eyes and a hood lurking somewhere in the background, at the edge of the woods. That was why we had all felt so watched. Every picture had some sort of ectoplasm in it, aside from a handful with an actual misty apparition. It showed me just how haunted and evil not only my home but my property was. I remembered what the woman who lived near me as a kid had taught me about ectoplasm in photos and what it meant but I decided to go and look it up for myself and spent days at the library

researching the subject and all about paranormal photos like the ones I had taken. I
know for a fact that the pictures were real and
after spending that time at the library I knew
what they really meant too. I moved six
months after purchasing the house but didn't
feel right about renting it and luckily I kept it
because I rent it out for paranormal investigations now and make a good living off it. The
photos I took so long ago are hanging all over
the walls. I retouched them and turned them
black and white, so that they would look a bit
more antique than they were, but it still
amazes me that I captured that much spirit
phenomenon on tape. The black shadow man is
still there and it seems he found a way inside
of the house now, instead of having to lurk at
the edges of the woods because he's the most
violent spirit in the home and the one I must
warn everyone about and the reason they must
sign such strict waivers. I know this story
doesn't seem very scary on the surface but
trust me, if you look up ectoplasm and what it
means when you see it in a photo and take

into consideration that the black shadow man was a hat man with glowing red eyes who downright attacked my friend and me, then you'll understand why this encounter story is quite horrifying. The home is infested and even though I rent it out I've only had one investigator come to me with one photo of an apparition he accidentally captured while he was in the house. I wonder why there's not as much being captured and I think it's because it's an intelligent haunting and therefore the spirits know that they can be captured if they aren't careful and that would only bring more people there. If there's one thing I know about lower vibrational spirits it's that they like to torment people and the more the merrier when they're concerned but they don't like paranormal investigators because if the right one finds out what it is and how to get rid of it then it's back to hell or wherever else for it, and obviously it doesn't want that.

Chapter 8

It Was A Shapeshifter

I've spent countless hours searching and scouring the internet looking for information on something unbelievable that I saw years ago, while walking along a deserted trail in the forest near my home. I was walking home from a friend's house and it was late at night. I was eighteen years old and still lived with my parents but I didn't have a curfew so I hadn't left my friend's house until around one in the morning. While you would never find me walking through deserted woods or anywhere else for that matter at that time of night now, it was something I did all the time back then. I had my license but was still saving up to buy

my first vehicle and my friend used her
parent's car and it wasn't available that night.
Even if I had been able to get a ride I probably
wouldn't have because I really enjoyed walking
through the forest. I loved listening to the
sounds of mother nature and all her animals
and insects and it was very calming for me. In
fact, even on nights when I was home and not
doing anything else, I would go for a walk
through the woods behind my house, which
were a part of the forest I was walking through
at the time of my encounter, and sometimes I
would be out there for an hour or more. I had
grown up in that house and knew that part of
the forest like the back of my hands and I had
become just as familiar with the trails that led
from my best friend's house to my parent's
house. It was a warm night and the moon was
full and it provided more than enough illumina-
tion for me to be able to see where I was
going.

To get from my friend's house to my own
there came a point about three quarters of the
way into the walk where I would have to cross

a two-lane road. The road was in the literal middle of nowhere and you would have to drive for almost an hour on it in either direction to get anywhere. It was just an old back country road and I had never seen any traffic on it at nighttime, whether I had been in a car and driving on it or walking across it going from one place to another on foot. It was incredibly quiet and I remember looking up at the moon and thinking of how lucky I was to live in a place as peaceful and beautiful as I did and how I didn't know what I would do if I didn't have those woods to walk through to clear my mind when I needed it. I still walk in the woods, camp, and hike, sometimes I even fish, when I'm in need of some clarity or just some peace and quiet. Just before I got to the road, about fifty feet from it, I started to feel as though I were being watched. I always got that feeling in that exact spot and it normally lasted until I crossed the road. Sometimes it would stay with me until I got home and there were even very rare occasions where I had gone into my house and upstairs into my bedroom, which overlooked the backyard and the forest beyond it, and I would still feel like there were eyes on me while I was standing by the window. When that happened, when the feeling followed me home I mean, I would always inevitably walk right upstairs and right to the window which I hadn't ever thought there was anything odd about until the night I'm telling you about now, when I realized it was very abnormal. There was something different about that time when I felt like I was being watched but I couldn't quite put my finger on what it was until about two minutes later it dawned on me. The whole forest seemed to have gone silent. It was incredibly eerie and I was immediately struck, for the first time, with how vulnerable I was out there. Cell phones didn't exist but even if they did I doubt there would have been much if any service in that area and it dawned on me that no one was around to hear me scream. That thought alone was so strange that it scared me but I kept trying to just keep walking and not get myself worked up. I quickened my pace a lot though and was walking fast instead of strolling like I normally would have been doing.

I was trying to make the silence make sense in my head and when I couldn't do that I knew I would need to try and distract myself or I would have had a meltdown right there in the woods because I had a bad habit of whipping myself into a panicked state for little to no reason at all. I started to sing out loud. It made me feel better for a minute but then I heard the telltale snap of a branch under someone's foot which gave away the fact that I wasn't alone out there as I had been so confident I was before the sound and that more than likely the reason I felt watched was because I was. I pretended like I didn't hear it so that I didn't give away that I had heard the branch snap to whoever was out there with me. I was always safe in the woods and never had any problems, even when it came to wild animals, but I did carry mace with me and I started to play with it in the pocket of my hoodie that I was wearing, getting it ready so that whoever it was couldn't see me and would be caught off guard and by surprise should they come any closer or God forbid try and attack me or something. I kept singing but my senses were heightened and I heard another branch snap. I stopped and turned around but at first I didn't see anything. I dropped all pretense of pretending no one was there and called out, asking who was there and telling them I had a large knife on me. Suddenly a cat came running out of the bushes over to the side of me where I had initially heard what I thought were steps. It stopped a few feet in front of me and started hissing and growling at me. It was creepy but I had to laugh because at that moment in time I thought that it had been the cat that had been snapping the branches. I hissed back at it and it turned and ran away. I continued walking, singing the whole way, until I eventually came to the two-lane road I had to cross.

I got to the road and stopped for a minute because I was listening to make sure that there was no one walking behind me and that it had in fact been the large cat. It was unusual for me to have seen a cat out there in the middle of nowhere and I was wondering where it could have come from in the first place. I guessed that someone driving along the road had abandoned the poor thing out there in the middle of nowhere. I heard it growling at me again from across the street and it was staring at me intensely, to the point where I got the chills and wished it would just go away. I told it that had it not been so mean that I would have scooped it up and taken it home and with that it hissed and went behind one of the trees where I could no longer see it, but not without hissing at me one last time. I looked both ways even though I knew there was no one coming and I crossed the road. I had taken about ten steps on the other side of the road, only enough to get into the woods and off what would have been considered the side of the road and heard a growling sound coming from behind me. I stopped in my tracks and my heart started to pound. It wasn't a cat that was behind me and I was sure that it wasn't any other kind of animal either. The thing about it was that it didn't sound like it was a human being either. I slowly turned around and looked and standing there was some sort of shadow figure. It was bipedal and stood at around five and a half feet tall. It was the same height as me. It looked mostly human except its ears were on the top of its head and looked like, well, they looked like a cat's ears. The eyes glowed green in the reflection of the moonlight, just as the large cat's had done a few moments earlier. I backed away slowly as it just stood there looking at me. I could see it watching me with its green cat's eyes but aside from those it had no other real features. I could see where the nose and mouth would have been but it was all shadow and nothing more. The forest was still eerily quiet.

I kept slowly backing away from it, careful not to trip over anything and end up in an even more vulnerable position than the one that I was already in and I kept looking back and down on the ground. The entity, or what-ever it was, hadn't moved yet but after I had taken about ten steps backwards it started to take a step towards me. I screamed at the top of my lungs but my voice only echoed through the trees and back towards me, just like I knew that it would. Suddenly I couldn't believe what I was hearing and the sound of a large truck speeding along the road broke the terror and the entity's gaze upon me. It looked from behind it where the road was to me and then back again and then, with one last glance back at me it turned and started running towards the road. It moved superhumanly quick and within the blink of an eye it was halfway across the road. I saw the headlights of the semi-truck that was speeding along the road. Large trucks like that weren't allowed on the road and I instantly wondered what the person was doing on the road to begin with, let alone traveling at such a fast speed. I heard the horn blare several times and watched in horror as the huge truck smashed right into the entity as it ran across the street. I heard a sickening thump accompanied by the sound of a cat squawking like it was in pain and then nothing but the engine as it grinded to a halt right after impact. I ran to the road and the guy got out yelling about how it came out of nowhere. I looked on the ground and there was a dead cat. It was almost unrecognizable and he didn't understand what it was that he had hit at first. He looked relieved when he saw it wasn't a person and I asked him if he was okay. He looked incredibly confused and kept looking from me to the dead animal that was splattered all over the road. He mumbled a few incoherent words but then got back in his truck and took off. How had that giant truck collided with a cat like that? Sure, it was a big cat, for as far as cats go, but it wasn't large enough to have collided with the truck's huge front end because it was high off the ground because of the wheels. I knew that he had seen the shadow person running across the road just like I had, and that he had thought that he hit a human being. He was probably drunk and just chalked it up to that and it was also the only reason I could think of why he left as quickly as he had.

The forest was alive and full of the usual

noises and animals again and there was no way I was going anywhere near where that cat/thing had been hit. The birds and insects, as well as the squirrels and other small animals were almost rejoicing at the death of the cat/being and I don't know why I thought I knew that but I did. I felt it, and that's the only way that I can explain it to you. I turned and started walking as fast as I could, still fingering the mace in my pockets, just in case. I got home and immediately went upstairs but didn't feel anything was watching me from the woods. Did the truck driver kill the entity by hitting it? How do you kill a paranormal creature? I know now that it was a shapeshifter but I wonder how that all works. I took a break from walking through the woods for a while but couldn't stay away from it forever. I had nightmares for months but then the memory just kind of went away. Recently I have been seeing a large cat, one that meows, growls and hisses just as viciously as the one I had seen all those years ago, staring at me and being nasty to me and my children as it stands at the edge of the treeline that separates my backyard and property from the woods. Is it the same entity? Has it somehow found me again after all these years? I honestly have no idea and don't even know if my shapeshifter explanation is what was going on but it's the best explanation I can come up with. That's all for now but I will keep you posted on my citation with the cat, provided anything to report should ever come up. Thanks for letting me get this off my chest.

Chapter 9

Terror in the Woods

I still have no idea what it was that I came across in the middle of the woods one rainy afternoon. I was a college student but I spent a lot of time when I was growing up camping, fishing, hiking, and I even did a little hunting with my dad. Hunting wasn't really my thing though I attempted it several times when my dad would want to go for us to spend some time together. My father was an avid outdoorsman and very experienced hunter and with his only child being me, a girl, he was always attempting to bond with me through the things he enjoyed the most. That was fine when I was younger but once I was older I started passing on the hunting trips but the rest of it I was eager to hang out with him and do. My father and I would go all over the state of Kentucky, which was where we lived and where I grew up and explore the depths of all the woodlands we could find. My grandparents owned a couple hundred acres out in the middle of nowhere and eventually that land got passed on to my father. I was spoiled, I won't lie, and my parents decided that since I was in college and working towards having my own career, that they would help me to be as self-sufficient as possible so I didn't marry for the wrong reasons. There's a lot that goes into that statement and choice that they made but it has nothing to do with the story except for the little house they built me on that property my dad got from my grandparents. I moved in after college and if you think about all the old-time fairy tales and the little houses the heroine or hero comes across literally in the middle of nowhere in a completely unexpected place in the middle of the forest, that would be the home they built for me there. My parents didn't live close and it would take them about two hours to get there when they would come and visit me and that's driving faster than the speed limit. I loved it and really did feel like I was living off the grid. I would be able to work from home and not have to deal with too many people. I had some social anxiety issues and all that. I had no neighbors and getting to my house would have been impossible for anyone who didn't know it was there. There's no way to drive up to it and there's also no reason for anyone to be wandering around out there because it's private property. There was a large swimming hole I liked to swim in the summer and that's kind of how this all started for me.

It was hot out one day and even though I had air conditioning I would rather be outside breathing in the fresh air instead of the artificial air that comes from those things. I hadn't thought of the swimming hole since I had moved in, which was about six months earlier, but I knew where it was because when my dad and I would camp on that land when I was little, we would camp right near it so that we could go swimming if the weather was nice. I went there and found it easily, remembering that there was a random bridge that didn't cross anything. It just hung there over the ground and was only about two hundred feet long. The bridge always gave me the creeps when I was little and I quickly realized that as an adult it made me feel the same way. I felt like the moment I stepped foot on the bridge something was watching me and it wasn't good. As soon as I would step off the bridge, whether that be on the other side or from just stepping off it because I didn't like the way I felt when I was on it, the feeling of being intensely watched by something evil would go right away immediately. I decided not to cross the weird bridge that day and just swim in the swimming hole. I must have gone out there almost every day for an entire two weeks before finally I decided to just camp out there for a weekend. I had checked the weather and it was supposed to be perfect camping weather, if not a little hot, all weekend long and so I packed up a few things and hiked out there to set up camp and relax. I camped near the bridge and swimming hole like my dad and I used to do so if it got too hot I would just be able to swim.

I spent my time hiking the land and just clearing my mind, organizing my thoughts but it felt different once the sun went down. Even on that first night, I was hiking back to my camp when the sun went down, and suddenly I felt like I wasn't alone. It was the exact same feelings as I always had while on the bridge but it was all around me and I wasn't near the bridge when the feelings came on. It was so intense that I stopped and shined my flashlight all around, even going so far as to call out and ask if anyone was there. The response I got made my heart skip a beat as a growling sound could be heard coming from all around me, in more than one spot. I didn't see anything though and so I hustled back to my camp and settled in for the night. I woke up at around two in the morning to use the bathroom and it was drizzling rain a little bit. I walked to the edge of the camp and into the trees a little bit to do my business and still felt like there were several sets of eyes on me. I was scared and I was beginning to think that maybe being out there at night wasn't the best idea. I hadn't considered that there could be anything that would or could hurt me out there because of all the time I spent camping as a child, both in those same woods and almost that exact same spot and so many other places all around the state. I had never been alone though and I thought maybe that was making me paranoid. I ran back to my tent but before I could get in I heard what I could have sworn was the sounds of a crying baby. I knew there was no way possible that there was a baby out there but the sound wasn't just in my head. It was very real and very much there and so I felt oblig- ated to go and look and see if someone was out there who maybe had a small baby with them and needed my help. It was coming from under the bridge. I walked to the bridge and shined my flashlight all around and under it but I didn't see anything. I had heard the crying infant right up to the point where I made it to the bridge and then I didn't hear anything. The feeling of being watched was more intense than ever before and I once again found myself running back to my tent because I was so afraid.

I tried my best to sleep that night. I got some sleep but it was restless. I woke up at around ten am and even though it was still drizzling, I decided to hike in the opposite direction from where I had always gone, on the trails with my dad. It was always to the right of that bridge and that day I decided to see what was on the left side of it. I noticed right away that the foliage and grass were over-grown on that side. It was almost comical the way it looked split down the middle like someone had been tending to one side and not the other. I didn't want to stay another night out there and figured I would just make the best of it and then head home. It was raining a little bit but I was prepared for that and I went on my way, planning on being out of the woods and back inside of my house by the time darkness fell. At first it was normal, except for feeling like I was being watched again but I had concluded that either the forest just felt that way or, as I said earlier, it was just all in my head because I had never been camping alone before. I was wearing a bright yellow poncho and had my little flashlight with me. I don't know what made me bring the flashlight but I'm glad that I did. It was only around one in the afternoon when I had my experience. I didn't only feel like I was being watched but I also kept hearing someone walking around my general vicinity. It was easy to hear as wet branches snapped harder because of the weather. The flora was incredibly unkempt and there was something so off putting about that area that I decided after only fifteen minutes of exploring there that I was going to turn around and go back to camp, pack everything up and head home. However, something else had other plans for me. I began to hear a baby crying again.

I looked all around and listened intently, trying to figure out where the sounds were

coming from. The fact that it could be something paranormal in nature never occurred to
me and so I knew in my mind that if I was
hearing a baby crying then there had to be a
baby crying somewhere. Once again I was led
back to the strange and creepy bridge. Of
course, after looking all around for about a
half hour, I didn't hear anything else and
hadn't found the source of the noise. Then, I
heard a little kid's voice calling out for help. It
felt distant but sounded like whoever it was
desperately needed someone's help. I yelled
out and asked, "where are you" and the
response that came back was, "over here!
Please help us!" My adrenaline was really
pumping at that point and I put two and two
together and realized that the child must have
been with the baby and that's why he or she
had said to help "us" as though there were
more than one. I went running in the direction
of the sound which took me away from the
swimming hole, past the bridge and into the
depths of the woods. I was completely out of
the clearing at that point. I was surrounded by

thick woods and I was scared but intent on finding the child or children and helping them. I called out again and got the same exact response but when following that noise, looking around in the trees and bushes, I heard something that made my heart almost stop. It was heavy breathing that had a growl attached to it as well. As I stood there breathing heavily, I heard whatever else was out there breathing heavily too and there was no way that it was a kid. It sounded large and the sense of evil I had been feeling on and off for the entirety of my trip was back and stronger than it had been up to that point. The fear I felt was almost debilitating. The rain was making it harder to see as it started pouring down on me to the point where I was becoming soaking wet. The child called for me one more time and I looked up in the direction where it was coming from. I could have sworn I had been right on top of it but it seemed like it had moved which would have been impossible because I had been standing right at the spot where I thought it had come from the first couple of times it called out to me.

I started to walk in that direction even though I didn't like the fact that it seemed as though I was being lured deeper and deeper through the woods with each step I took and each time the helpless child called to me. Just as I was heading into the forest deeper than I had ever been before, I saw something slightly move out of the corner of my eye. I needed to look at it but I didn't want it to be obvious. I kept looking all around, trying to catch a good glimpse of it out of my peripheral vision. I heard the child calling again, more desperate than ever before, and it was coming from where I had seen the movement. I turned very quickly to face whatever was there, part of me still thinking I was dealing with a child and possibly a baby and another part of me knowing that something was just trying to lure me out there. I immediately saw glowing red eyes and a tall black shadow. It knew I had seen it and it stepped out from behind the trees. "Help us!" it said, though it didn't have any features so it didn't have a mouth that moved. It had been projecting its voice the whole time to get me to wander deeper and deeper into those woods. When I looked at it again it growled and I turned and ran as quickly as I could back to my house, leaving everything that I had brought with me there in the woods. As I ran I would catch glimpses of the shadow person with the red eyes all along the way, and when I passed the bridge I heard the baby crying in pain again. I stopped for just a second and looked and the shadow being was there too. I screamed and ran and it followed me. I made it out of the woods and into my backyard and that's when I heard an animalistic howling/screaming sound that echoed all over the place.

The strangest part is that as soon as I stepped out of the woods and into my yard, there was no more rain. It was suddenly a bright and sunny, somewhat hot, and humid day. The ground wasn't wet and the sky wasn't dark. I ran inside and locked the doors and watched from the window the shadow people, ten that I counted, watching me. None of them stepped out of the forest though and I never went back into it again. I stayed in the house for a long time and have had many people come in and go into the forest to do investigations but none of them have been able to come up with anything new. I was dealing with something evil and possibly demonic, called a mimic, that was trying to play on my heart strings by using the voices of a small child and crying baby to get me to go deeper and deeper into the woods. Once I laid eyes on it, which everyone agreed that it wasn't expecting, it could no longer hide itself and that's when I started seeing the shadow people. However, one last terrifying part to my encounter is that almost all the professionals I brought in told me that the shadows with the red eyes weren't the true face of the creatures either. I was taught how to do protective mechanisms to set up boundaries between my yard and the woods to keep them off my property and out of my home and personal space and it worked for years. I wasn't allowed to sell the house because it wasn't mine and my parents didn't believe anything I told them and thought it was all a side effect from being overworked and isolated all the time. That's all I know and I'll be writing about a few more things that seem like they could be paranormal too that never occurred to me until all of this happened, that took place when my dad and I were there when I was growing up. Thanks for letting me share and I hope this makes sense to anyone reading it. Because there are so many unknowns, sometimes it's very hard to explain to someone who has never experienced something similar.

Chapter 10

Echos From the Glen

In the early 2000s, the haunting allure of the supernatural, combined with the raw sting of heartbreak, propelled me into a journey unlike any other. I had meticulously planned a trip to a secluded lodge in the rugged embrace of the Scottish Highlands. This whole endeavor was originally a love letter to my fiancée, a shared dream birthed from our mutual fascination with ghostly tales. Yet, fate, being the unpredictable force that it is, made us tread different paths before I could surprise her with our dream getaway.

Undeterred by the gnawing void of her absence, I ventured forth. Perhaps it was a need to fill the emptiness or to seek closure. The vast expanse of the Highlands seemed both liberating and isolating. The final leg of my trip was a lonesome drive, crisscrossing through the unpredictable mountainous terrain. The lodge itself was a paradox, encapsulating tranquility against a backdrop that whispered tales of ancient battles and spectral entities.

The previous guests had shared their tales, weaving a tapestry of legends. This lodge was not just a mere structure; it was a relic, having once been a sanctuary for Highland warriors during tumultuous times. The onset of ghostly disturbances coincided with the renovations undertaken by its new custodians. My chosen chamber was whispered to be at the heart of these supernatural occurrences.

The first anomaly was the forest outside my window, which would transform from a picturesque landscape during daylight to a haunting silhouette in the night. Yet, even before the sun had set, the room serenaded me with soft whispers, emanating from shadowed corners and vanishing as quickly as they came.

The pain of my heartbreak seemed to intertwine with the lodge's melancholy. I imagined how different it would be had she been by my side, lending me courage.

As night tightened its grip, an even more terrifying manifestation occurred. The room's closet, which I had earlier checked and found to be ordinary, creaked open. It revealed a pair of malevolent, crimson eyes, shimmering in the semi-darkness. With the room now feeling like a cage, I sought solace in the vastness of the forest outside.

Navigating the labyrinth of trees and underbrush by the slender moonlight, a persistent feeling of being observed made my spine tingle. A rancid smell, echoing the charred remains of a battlefield, made me gag. The whispers, now accompanied by eerie lullabies, played tricks with my mind.

The climax of my terror came when a shadowy figure, towering and draped in tattered robes, emerged from the dense fog.

Its face, an unsettling canvas of charred and pallid skin, sent chills down my spine. Those same red eyes, now set in a grotesque face, bore into mine. Its shriek, piercing the night, seemed like a war cry from a forgotten age.

Pushed to my limits, I bolted back towards the lodge, feeling as if the entire forest and its phantoms were in pursuit. Safely inside, the whispers and eerie lullabies continued their relentless torment until dawn's first light.

The sun's rays brought sanity, and with a heavy heart, I packed my memories alongside my belongings. As I left the lodge behind, the Highlands seemed to sigh, as if letting go of a long-held secret. My chilling experience, now a testament to the spectral realm, took years to muster the courage to share, a tale of love, loss, and haunted landscapes.

Chapter 11

The Curse of Elderwood Forest

Since childhood, Adrian was captivated by the mysterious and the unexplained. By the age of five, he was engrossed in thrillers, and his parents didn't see any harm, often shielding his eyes during the intense scenes. Unlike many, he never let his fears govern his actions or thoughts. So, when he enrolled in a multimedia course during his high school years in the quaint town of Norfield, he was constantly producing thriller-inspired content. Soon, his mentor Mr. Thompson urged him to explore other genres, given that every project Adrian submitted had an eerie undertone.

All these early experiences were precursors to Adrian's brush with the supernatural. Though he had some odd experiences in the past, he could never conclusively label them as paranormal. However, his undying curiosity led him to investigate the fabled tale of Elara, the Elderwood Enchantress. Legends whispered about how Elara was executed in the 1500s for her mystical practices, leading her to curse the Elderwood forests.

Adrian's interest piqued when he stumbled upon old diaries and sketches at Norfield's community library – this was a time before the internet era. Being in his early twenties, with a gap year and a part-time job at his aunt's bookstore, he had the luxury of time. Determined to explore Elderwood overnight, he sought company, but his friends declined, wary of the stringent trespassing laws in Elderwood. His girlfriend, Clara, although supportive, wasn't keen on joining because of her own phobias.

Following some research, and against Clara's

advice, Adrian decided to use an Ouija board as a medium to communicate with any lurking spirits. Back in the early '70s, these boards were marketed as harmless children's games. Unbeknownst to Adrian, the board would be the gateway to his most chilling experience.

Upon entering Elderwood, a looming dread overcame his initial enthusiasm. He recorded any potential sounds or events with a vintage tape recorder, a gift from his lawyer father. Midnight approached, and under the soft glow of a candle, Adrian tentatively used the Ouija board. To his alarm, the planchette moved wildly, repeatedly spelling out "GO" before finally spelling out, "Bound to me."

Chilled to the bone and regretting his choices, Adrian decided to retreat. But as he journeyed deeper into the forest, harrowing screams resonated around him. Every horror movie he had seen couldn't have prepared him for this.

Despite his terror, exhaustion overtook him, and he found himself in a troubled sleep. His nightmares soon became reality when he awoke to face Elara herself. Floating eerily, her age-lined face, contorted in malice, reflected the legend. Her ghastly presence was intensified by shadows that danced around her, flitting between the trees. The entity's intent was clear – she wanted Adrian.

In a desperate bid to escape, Adrian dashed through the forest, with Elara's shrill cries echoing behind him. Upon reaching the fringes of Elderwood, he noted the enchantress wouldn't cross the boundary. This marked the end of his ordeal for the night, but it was only the beginning of a haunting that would last for years.

Returning to Norfield, he sought answers in the town's records. Detailed sketches confirmed his terrifying encounter with Elara. But the tape recorder, left behind in his haste, held potentially even more revealing evidence.

Adrian moved on with his life, but the shadowy figures he'd seen in Elderwood continued to make appearances, especially during his nightmarish replays of that evening.

His tale serves as a chilling reminder of the boundaries between our world and the unknown — and the consequences of crossing them.

* * *

CONTINUE WITH

13 PAST MIDNIGHT: VOLUME 2

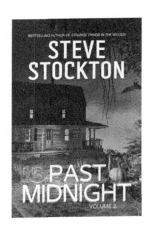

About the Author

Steve Stockton is a veteran outdoorsman and author who has been investigating the unexplained for over 35 years. Originally from the mountains of East Tennessee, Steve has traveled all over the country and many parts of the world and now makes his home in picturesque New England with his wife, Nicole, and their dog, Mulder.

Steve cites his influences as his "gypsy witch" grandmother, who told him multitudes of legends and stories as a small child, as well as authors such as Frank Edwards, John Keel, Charles Fort, Loren Coleman, Ivan Sanderson, Colin Wilson, and Nick Redfern.

His published books include Strange Things in the Woods (a collection of true, paranormal encounters) as well as the autobiographical My Strange World, where he talks about his own experiences dating back to childhood. Recently, he has written National Park Mysteries and Disappearances, Volumes 1, 2, and 3.

He also owns and narrates the wildly popular Among The Missing Youtube channel.

Also by Steve Stockton

MYSTERIES IN THE DARK

STRANGE THINGS IN THE WOODS

NATIONAL PARK MYSTERIES & DISAPPEARANCES

MY STRANGE WORLD

Also by Free Reign Publishing

Made in United States
Orlando, FL
16 September 2024

51550576R00086